HOW TO FIND YOUR UNIQUE ART STYLE

Dorothy Murgatroyd

Dorothy Murgatroyd

For more information, address: dmurgatroydart@gmail.com

First edition March 2022

Book design by Dorothy Murgatroyd
(thanks Canva, Pixlr and Pixabay!)

ISBN 978-0-473-62353-1

www.dmurgatroydart.wordpress.com

To my mother and my husband:
Thank you for your belief in me as an artist

CONTENTS

1. DO YOU KNOW YOURSELF?

Why Do you Make Art?

Finding your "why" is incredibly important for finding your style.

If you are wanting to communicate to street kids via art, you might decide to become a street artist and learn graffiti art to reach your target audience.

Do you have something to say and communicate? One of my concerns is the way we steward our environment so nature is often a theme in my art.

Do you want to make money from your art? Alternatively, are you happy to have it as a hobby that refreshes you?

Is it the social connection that you are looking for through art?

Is it the processing of life and emotions?

So:

who is your intended audience?

- just you
- a target audience
- friends and family

Again, why do you make art?

Is it for:

- Processing life and emotions?
- Money?
- Communication of a message?
- To connect with like-minded arty friends.
- For fun and refreshment?
- For giving - either personally as gifts (cards and artworks etc.) or as a larger gift to the community (e.g., murals and enhancing community spaces). Or to create funds to give out of?
- For illustrating - books or other projects.

- For decorating your own space.

Set some intentions for your art

I'm guessing if you're reading this book one of your goals is to find your style.

Take time out as you read this book to write down your intentions in the free printable workbook that is linked in the back of the book or in a notebook.

Why do you want to make art?

I encourage you to think about *why* you want to make art.

For myself, after reading Simon Sinek's book "*Find Your Why*", I realised that my "why" in art is:

"To restore beauty in places and people (particularly the poor and broken -hearted) so that God's glory and beauty are seen again in them."

How this effects my art style:

Where possible, I am drawn to renovate old canvases - to rescue them!

I am drawn to art journaling in the area of the healing of emotions. This is not art to sell, or for public display but to heal the soul. It is a raw product for me and anyone who works with me in art journaling classes will be producing a style that is raw and not always finished but conveys emotion. The papers used can be non-archival and the mediums not permanent.

If I am working on a project of raising money to restore people or places, then that style of art I create to sell will be finished and planned and on quality materials and using higher quality products.

If I am using art to play and experiment, that will be more likely to be in sketchbook format. It may not be in my usual style but may be incorporated into my style if I like the results. (For example, exploring a new medium like Neo colour crayons).

Often the phrase " I want
to make art to.................... so
that..."
can help you with where to start.

In the first line put your contribution to others through your art, on the second line put the impact of your contribution.

For example my why for this book:

"I want to write an art style help book so that other artists don't have to spend years searching for theirs (as I have done)."

Check out your workbook now for the fill in the phrase exercise.

What are your goals for your art?

List them out and the different why's behind them to bring clarity to your art projects and bring some more light to your style.

2. KNOW WHAT YOU LIKE

What are the colours you have around you already?

- What are the colours you wear? What is your favourite colour?
- What are the colours you have around you already?
- Do you and your family or flatmates agree on favourite colours? (That's if you live with others). When they give feedback on your art it may be determined on what colours they like!
- Thinking about the colours below, which would you choose? Choose at least 3

Know What you Like Exercise:

- Create a tiny artwork in a square, 4" by 4" or about 10cm by 10cm. Use the 3 colours you picked above. I suggest you use one colour (your favourite) for about 3/4 of the square, and the other 2 colours in the remaining 1/4 of the square.

This is an example with blue dominating my artwork.

N.Z. Clematis by D. Murgatroyd

- Create a second artwork in the same dimensions using 3 of your least favourite colours as above - like a mirror image or very similar image. (Or take a photo as I did and use the colour tools in your favourite photo editing programme to change the colours digitally).

Pixlr is a free online picture editing tool you could try:

https://pixlr.com/th/e/

Here I have taken my first artwork and digitally changed it to sepia or brown tones (one of my least used colours as I can tell from all the tubes of unused brown paint that I have stockpiled!)

From the chart below, write in the season names of the 3 colours you chose. For example; if you chose the first box; yellow, the corresponding chart identifies it as a Spring/Autumn colour.

yellow	mauve	cobalt	red	cyan
emerald	green	indigo	lime	magenta
teal	olive	violet	ſienna	crimſon
pink	ſteel	brown	orange	amber

spring/ autumn	summer	winter/ sum-mer	winter	summer / winter
summer / winter	summer	winter	spring/ autumn	winter
spring	autumn/ spring	winter	summer / winter	autumn
summer	summer / winter	autumn	autumn	autumn/ spring

- Are the colours you chose all from the same season?

- Are they both summer and winter (cooler colours on the spectrum)?

- Or are they both Autumn and Spring (warmer colours on the spectrum)? Or are they a mix of the seasons?

This is a starting point to think about what colours you prefer. I find it hard to like artworks I make outside of what I personally like colour wise.

Most people are drawn to either the cool colours on the spectrum (Summer/Winter colours) or the warm colours (Autumn/Spring).

Do you fit this pattern? Are you drawn to warmer or cooler colours? I haven't added white into this colour selection as whites can have warm or cool tints.

Looking at your mini artworks does this pattern fit? If not, can you work out why?

3. WHAT TYPE OF ART DO YOU PREFER?

What is your favourite art style?

Rank these art styles from least liked to loved: (add any art style that you like that is not there to the list)

- graphic (including cartoon type art) art outlined with line and very clean looking?
- graffiti (or street art) including stencil art
- abstract -very painterly (including fluid art painting) -
- abstract geometric
- classic - realism, historical artworks, photorealism
- folk art
- midcentury
- shaker

- Retro
- narrative art/ comic styled art
- Tribal/ indigenous art
- modern (including surrealism, cubism, fantasy,)
- patterned
- impressionistic
- other ....

Your next exercise is to create an artwork in your favourite style:

Keeping it simple: the guidelines are "something botanical, using monochromatic colours."

Monochromatic colours are one colour plus white and black.

Create it in a format of an A5 piece of paper.

Then create an artwork in your least favourite style that is also monochromatic and in the small format of an A5. (148 x 210 mm or 5.8 x 8.3 inches)

Compare your reactions to these two artworks - do you favour the style you prefer? Or were you surprised into liking a non favourite style?

What is your favourite format?

Your next art exercise is to make different shapes of art The shapes are circular, square, rectangular, oval, diamond, cross and hexagonal. If there is another shape that comes to mind that you want to trial add it also.

To simplify this exercise, and give you a starting point, the idea prompt is to use collage or digital art to create these pieces, with a landscape theme if you're stuck for ideas.

Examples of experimenting with digital art in a different shape format. Try putting your art into a digital editing programme and then create a mask or shape.

Even cropping an image can make a new shape such as rectangular to square.

Digital image D Murgatroyd ©2016

Example of collage art with the landscape theme:

Memory Landscape 2 by D. Murgatroyd © 2020

An easy way to create a cross canvas is to glue 2 small box canvases to a rectangular main section. This way you can experiment to see if you like this format before investing in more expensive shaped canvases or wood.

What size is your workspace?

Your preferred art size could also determine the amount of space you need for your workspace., unless the weather is very temperate where you are and you are able to work outside for periods of time.

- Do you like to make small art or larger artworks or something in between? What kind of space do you already have to work in?
- Are you working in a tiny home or travelling? Or do you have your own space in the garage or studio and can work large?
- Are you O.K. with working from the kitchen table and continually packing your art supplies up on a daily basis?
- Do you have kids and need to protect your art? (Also the need to protect your children from possibly toxic art supplies is another consideration). Do you need to have a separate art space?
- Can you work with people around or do you like to work in solitude?

Exercises to explore your art size preferences:

- Make a piece of tiny art (inchies are 1" by 1", twinchies are 2" by 2").

When my art season is one of constraint whether time wise or space wise, "inchies" or tiny art pieces are my go to so I can keep my creative practice alive.

In this demonstration piece I cut out a 2-inch square piece of painted paper and then collaged some scraps on top, finished off by line work with a sharpie pen.

- Make a piece of art that is the largest scale you can fit into your floor space, outdoor space (if it's not raining), or table space. You could even try beach art!

Beach art by Tauranga artist Zane McGregor photo D. Murgatroyd

- Make a piece of art that is medium size

Textures you prefer

Another question to ask yourself is what texture do I prefer?

Some artists prefer to work on a smooth surface and others love laying gesso and collage to make a highly textured surface.

Where are you on the texture spectrum? Does it depend on the project?

Here are two exercises to investigate this:

- Take a smooth surface paper and spill some coffee or tea on it. Take some watercolours and put some puddles of paint on the page too. Now draw into this with watercolour pencils or water-soluble media such as neo colour crayons or even charcoal.
- Now, take another piece of paper and scrape gesso across it with a credit card or piece of cut plastic. Glue on some scraps of paper or magazines, next find some textured material to glue on.

  Now, draw into this surface.

Which do you prefer?

Mind Map session:

Mind mapping is a great tool for discovering what you like.

You start with a central bubble with the question "What do I like?"

You can then branch out from there and add

questions such as these ones:

- preferred colours (warm/cool)
- styles
- sizes
- working alone or in groups
- messy art versus non messy art (this may determine your mediums for example I don't like charcoal and pastels due to the messiness)
- smells (e.g. some people don't like the fumes of real oil paints)
- who you wish you could paint like?
- what you would buy in an art gallery with unlimited funds
- favourite textures
- favourite shapes
- art that you hate
- what type of house style you have?
- any other art investigations

Mind Map

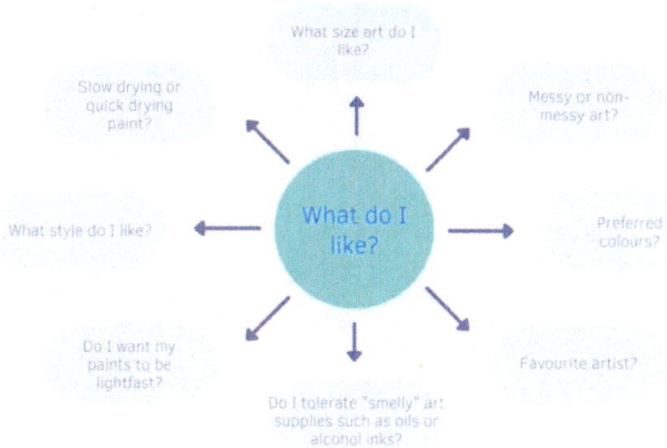

This is an example of a digital mind map created on Canva

Digital mind map resources for free:

Canva (free version has 4 mind map templates, and you can invite others to collaborate).

https://www.canva.com/graphs/mind-maps/

Coggle (free version has 3 private diagrams to try)

https://coggle.it/

MindMup (free version has unlimited mind maps with export options of up to 100KB, and storage for up to 6 months)

https://www.mindmup.com/

4. KNOW WHAT YOU DISLIKE

Make Some Bad Art!

Yes, I'm telling you to make some bad art! (Or maybe you already have some). You then need to work out why you don't like this art. For some people working out what they don't like helps direct them to a style they do like! Feel free to skip this step if you are already becoming a lot clearer on what you like style wise.

Critique Sheet :

- Do I like the colours? yes/no
- Do I like the shapes? yes/no

- Do I like the textures? yes/no

- Do I like the contrast? yes/no

- Do I like the layout/composition? yes/no

- Do I like the percentages of colours? yes/no

- Can you then alter your “bad art” using this feedback?

An example of "ugly art" in colours I dislike

Although I still dislike the colours, I like the improved contrast on these pieces using ink and marks I like.

5. INSPIRATION

Creating a mood board

Where do you get your inspiration from?

What inspires you? (It will be unique to you and be a part of your style).

For example, I am not interested in trucks, so my style is highly unlikely to be using the theme of trucking! I am interested in birds so my artwork themes will often include birds, feathers and their environment.

Wikipedia's description of a mood board:

"A **mood board** is a type of visual presentation or 'collage' consisting of images, text, and samples of objects in a composition. It can be based on a set topic or can be any material chosen at random. A mood board can be used to convey a general idea or feeling about a particular topic."

Exercise: Make a mood board physically
or on Pinterest or on Canva

https://www.canva.com/create/mood-boards/

How to make a physical mood board:

- Choose a limited number of colours - start with 3 colours plus white and black. Paint shops have colour cards if you need inspiration and often their test pots are a great way to play with new paint ideas, premixed and repeatable! If you're bored and needing a change : buy a test pot in a metallic paint colour!

- Choose 5 keywords - what are you interested in currently? (Try the website "generator fun" for a random word generator if you're really stuck!)

https://generatorfun.com/generators

- Choose 3 patterns you like

- Choose your supplies: magazines or print outs of images that relate to the above colours and keywords. Gather a glue stick or tape, scissors, and a surface to stick your images to

- Cut out pictures and words that inspire you and arrange them a s a collage on a sheet at least A4 size or bigger. Try having a least one larger key image and smaller supporting ones.

Creating a digital mood board

You can create one in pages if you have a Mac or Windows if you have a PC. or use Evernote (a free basic program for note taking)

Simply copy and paste images into your document and arrange them. Print them out if you want to have it on the wall for inspiration.

There are also a couple of websites such as Pinterest and Canva and Milanote where you can sign up for a free account and create a savable online mood board. (Print it off if you want a hard copy)

Artist dates:

Go to a gallery, sculpture park, museum, circus, fun park, local agricultural farm show, anything new to you.

Find your inspirational place.

Jane Cameron in the book “The Artist’s Way” explains why we need artist dates. In a nutshell: input in equals output. No input means your inspiration will eventually dry up.

Getting to know what inspires you is part of your style formula.

Here are some ideas to try:

- Either find a gallery nearby or an online one that you can go to for inspiration.

If they have a brochure - get one and use it on your inspiration board, or if you have time do a few quick sketches and notes of what inspires you to make some art after visiting the gallery.

- Find a sculpture park - take photos or make some sketches

- Give yourself some small change to go second-hand shopping - things to look out for: interesting textures for making things, preloved books to turn into art journals or collage, more art supplies, etc.

- Go for a nature walk - collect leaves, take photos or sketches, do bark rubbings. This is an example of a little book inspired by lichen and bark:

- Go for a city walk - see if there is a street art trail or take rubbings from interesting objects, find interesting textures and photograph them

- Buy a new art supply to play with

- Buy a new food - draw it first then eat it!

An example of an artist's date I did during a COVID lockdown was going on a virtual art gallery tour of the Napier Museum called MTG Hawkes Bay.

https://collection.mtghawkesbay.com/explore

This is a beautiful artwork that I found (among many other inspiring art works and objects):

https://collection.mtghawkesbay.com/objects/37256/white-wings

I used this picture to think about my art style and learn from a true master of art, studying in particular his composition for this artwork.

I then experimented in my art journal:

Journal page inspired by "White Wings" by Leo Bestall

Idea Inspiration:

I created this list for my daughter who was needing inspiration for her school art board:

What are you passionate about?

What movie have you watched that impacted you emotionally?

What about a poem?

Or a book?

A song that emotionally impacts you?

Or what is it in the world that makes you sad or mad that you would like to change?

What thing would you like to speak on if you gave a speech?

Or is there a news item that upsets you?

Or a belief you want to communicate?

A thought you'd like to challenge?

A story you'd like to tell?

6. STRETCHING YOURSELF

Why stretch yourself? Because this way, you will find out whether you like something or not.

Like developing in food preferences, you develop your tastes by eating something different and you develop your art tastes by trying new things!

Goal: to try a new media to see if you like it and want to incorporate it into your style.

Use food as a theme prompt:

- create an artwork using a medium (what goes on your paper/substrate) you haven't used before.

It could even be food colouring while we're on the food theme, or natural pigments such as tea and coffee or turmeric or beetroot juice! However, as most food based paints are not light fast, I would not recommend them for any artworks of permanence. In my experiments, they often reacted to the acidity of the paper and changed colour over time.

An example of experimental art in my art journal, the left page was created with a stencil painted with coffee.

7. PRODUCTIVITY

The more art you make, the more your style will develop **if** you follow this formula:

"Practice + time + intention+feedback =style"

Everyone knows what time and practice mean, but what about intention?

Intention

Intention is the ability to set goals and measure your output by those goals.

For example, you learned to do handwriting by practice plus time plus your teacher's intention that it be of a certain size, slope, shape, speed, spacing and using a sharp pencil! (The six "S's" of handwriting). If you have retaught yourself writing, for example, in calligraphy or lettering, you would have used the same process. After time, your writing style will become automatic and personalised.

Practice

Practice is to do with repetition. The more you repeat an action the more automatic it will get. If you want to get better at that action, that is where feedback and intention come in.

Feedback

Make sure you are getting some feedback either from yourself or, preferably, from someone further along the art path than you. This is where you don't just want a course you want an art course with personal feedback.

Time

I heard an excellent tip on building new habits. It was: ***schedule it***.
If it isn't scheduled it won't happen. If you say "I'll make some art ", chances are, it won't happen. If

you say, “I'll make some art on my bed, doodling for 10 minutes before lights out.”, it's far more likely to happen.

Your turn to apply this:

Intention : Look back at Chapter one and your goals.

What one goal out of these could you work toward? Take one thing and work towards it. For example; finding a colour palette that is you or a certain look you're going for for example; retro, mid-century, shaker, minimalist.

Take the worksheet below and print it out for a before and after recording if you want to see your progress!

Worksheet:

Starting date: ______________

Goal:____
____
____
____
______

Scheduled time to work on this:______________________

Finishing date:
____

Feedback on goal_________________________________
____
____
____
____

Productivity from accountability

Accountability equals people in your life! We grow via relationship.

Another way to increase productivity for some personality types will be art community challenges. I know from myself the posting on Instagram and feedback from the people on Instagram made a big difference in my daily creativity. (Shout out to my Instagram friends- thank you!)

However, there is a point where social media becomes a distraction and a negative feedback loop (via comparison) and not a help and you have to monitor that for yourself. Occasionally, I will take a technology fast which can help you refocus as to why you're on social media.

Some people join a real-life art group in their area for accountability and growth. Art groups often have exhibition dates which can be a deadline to work towards (if you understand the Meyers-Briggs personality test and are a P you will need deadlines to get art made!). See online tests if you want to find out what you are in personality type. It may even help you with your style as you will again, know yourself better!

Just make sure that the art challenge/art group is in line with you overall goals. For example, I need to balance out fun art with more serious art goals so 15 minutes fun on an art challenge is doable if I'm also working toward my larger art goals.

There are lots of challenges out there. If you put in the search for an art challenge on Instagram you should come up with a plenty.

Happily, there is always some challenge to be involved in whenever you start. It is a lovely way of meeting online artists. I even created my own Instagram challenge once and met some lovely artists via it.

If you're not interested in challenges another way of increasing productivity would to be taking a class. Art classes are available online and in person and most are doable at your own pace.

No group in your area? Set up your own! Invite some friends over for some art fun together - just put out a large plastic tablecloth and get everyone to bring non messy supplies or help with cleanup.

Simplify to increase productivity

One of my goals is to try to be creative everyday - even if it is just a quick doodle on paper! If you keep your supplies simple (pen and sketchbook next to your bed) this will make it extremely doable.

Limiting supplies will increase your productivity

Simplify. Find your style by limiting time, supplies, colours, and size of art.

Simplify your colour choices

- Create a limited palette.

Exercises:

- create a colour palette collection sketchbook

Here's an example of a palette created by collecting colours together from scraps of paper and then working out the matching colours from them:

I suggest finding colours that have both light and dark tones for your palette (Take a digital photo of your colours and then change the colours to black and white in your photo app to be able to see the tones).

Exercise 1

Try and limit your palette to 3 colours plus black and white and see what happens

Exercise 2

Try collecting 5 colours from scrap paper or magazines and then try and create those colours to make a palette

Exercise 3

Paint stripes of colours together to see how they can affect each other - make some larger or wider and some thinner and smaller

Exercise 4

Go on a colour hunt around your neighbourhood with your phone or camera and see if you can get palette inspiration from your photos

Style can also be worked out from what you don't include!

Simplicity may be your style. For example; try leaving more white space as an exercise.

Do you like what you have created?

8. BORROWING FROM HISTORICAL ARTISTS OR ARTIST MOVEMENTS

In Austin Kleon's book *Steal Like An Artist* he shares a great insight, "What a good artist understands is that nothing comes from nowhere. All creative work builds on what came before. Nothing is completely original."

What I want you to look back on is your mind map or quiz in Chapter one and have a look at historical art movements or historical artists you prefer.

From that, choose 2 artists who you like. Choose a painting from each to work from. These will inspire you to create some art.

For the first artwork:

- choose the same colour palette as your chosen artwork but change up the composition.

For the second artwork:

- choose the same composition as your chosen artwork but a different palette.

To speed up the process feel free to trace over the main composition lines, this is not a drawing practice unless you want to make it one. The focus is finding a style.

Changing up the colour palette but keeping the composition the same:

My sketchbook example from William Turner's "Snow Storm: Steam-Boat off a Harbour's Mouth":

Final abstract sketch from my sketchbook more in "my style" at the time

For the third artwork:

- try and combine something of each!

Remember - you're allowed to make bad art on the way to discovering the art you love to make!

For extra credit, look at the themes of the artwork you have picked and create your own art using one of these themes.

Outline exercises from historical art:

OUTLINE EXERCISE 1. Historical artist to study: Van Gogh. He sometimes outlines his art as the values between sections may not bring enough clarity. Try out a piece with outlines around each object - do you like the results?

Thatched Cottages at Cordeville
Painting by Vincent van Gogh

OUTLINE EXERCISE 2. Painting outside the lines. For example the artist Dufy.

Regatta at Cowes By Raoul Dufy (1877-1953), Fair use, https://en.wikipedia.org/w/index.php?curid=1917548

Create blocks of colour and then draw lines or the other way around!

Do you like this style?

OUTLINE EXERCISE 3. Use a variety of line/no outlines - e.g., Matisse:

He uses a very patterned style in the painting "Landscape at Collioure" with no outlining at all.

Try experimenting with this style in this exercise.

Landscape at Collioure By Henri Matisse - MoMA, PD-US, https://en.wikipedia.org/w/index.php?curid=21463164

Consider the thickness of the line, colour, and consistency.

OUTLINE EXERCISE 4. Try using different coloured outlines.

Try a colour other than black for outlining your shapes. You could also try broken lines, or patterned lines.

White outlines are demonstrated in this artwork:

N.Z. Iris or Mikoikoi by D. Murgatroyd © 2017

Borrowing from current Artists or art movements

Current art moments are:

- Digital art e.g., David Hockney
- Fluid Art
- Art in your local art gallery
- Street art

Other new art forms to investigate if you have the appropriate tools are 3D motion graphics, crypto art, and neon art (created with neon lighting).

9. IMPROVE AN ARTWORK RECIPE

- Turn your image into black and white by taking a photo. Is there enough contrast or does it all look the same tone?

- Does it have enough strong darks and bright lights?

- Put your image into a colour percentage tool or visually assess it? The website below analyses your colours for free:

  http://mkweb.bcgsc.ca/color-summarizer/?home

Perseverance 2 (teasel) by D. Murgatroyd © 2019

THE IMAGE IN WORDS

bay blue botticelli breaker cadet cerulean chateau comet cool crisp dolphin endorphin eskimo forecast green grey gull gumbo hippie hit moderate nepal pale shakespeare steel teal turquoise undercover

COLOR CLUSTERS

Colors in the image were clustered into 5 groups (k-means). The average color of the colors for each cluster is shown. The name is the closest named color and its distance is shown using ΔE. The tags are the set of words formed by all named neighbours within ΔE ≤ 5. The list of words above is the set of all unique words in this set of words.

Cluster colors, sized by number of pixels:

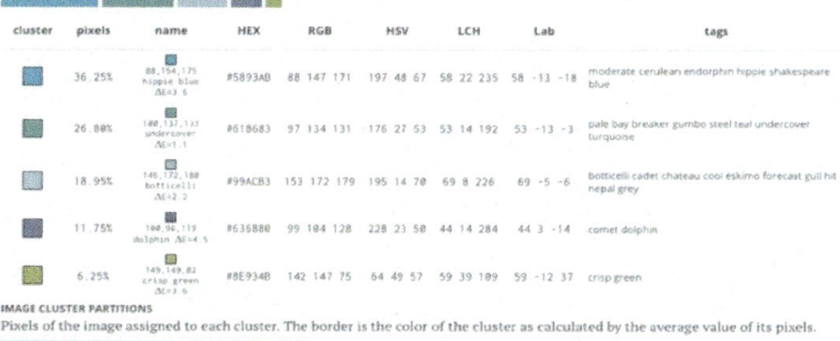

cluster	pixels	name	HEX	RGB	HSV	LCH	Lab	tags
	36.25%	88,154,175 hippie blue ΔE=3.6	#5893AB	88 147 171	197 48 67	58 22 235	58 -13 -18	moderate cerulean endorphin hippie shakespeare blue
	26.80%	100,137,133 undercover ΔE=1.1	#618683	97 134 131	176 27 53	53 14 192	53 -13 -3	pale bay breaker gumbo steel teal undercover turquoise
	18.95%	146,172,180 botticelli ΔE=2.2	#99ACB3	153 172 179	195 14 70	69 8 226	69 -5 -6	botticelli cadet chateau cool eskimo forecast gull hit nepal grey
	11.75%	100,96,119 dolphin ΔE=4.5	#636880	99 104 128	228 23 50	44 14 284	44 3 -14	comet dolphin
	6.25%	149,149,82 crisp green ΔE=3.6	#8E934B	142 147 75	64 49 57	59 39 109	59 -12 37	crisp green

IMAGE CLUSTER PARTITIONS

Pixels of the image assigned to each cluster. The border is the color of the cluster as calculated by the average value of its pixels.

Colour percentages from website mentioned above

Another really helpful website (particularly if you are in New Zealand or Australia) is the Resene Colour Palette Generator:

Resene Colour Palette Generator

You can put your artwork in and see your percentages. Also very useful is the fact that you can find matching paint colours if you want to decorate a room in similar colours. This is particularly helpful with commissions as your clients can then match their decorating schemes easily.

Working backwards, as I did with one commission, you can take photos of the clients current colour scheme (cushions, couches, wall colours etc.) and then create matching artworks using Resene paints. This worked exceptionally well for me.

- Is there a dominant colour you can recognise?

The chart above shows colour dominance of 36% for my main colour, closely followed by a very similar colour of 26%. Adding these together gives me a 62% colour dominance. The goal for a really strong colour recipe is main colour dominance of about 70%.

- Is there a left-hand entrance point for the eye? (This is for Western art). This could be a strong dark or light or a contrasting colour.

- Is the focal point in an interesting place?

- Do lines lead to the focal point?

- 1/3 to 2/3 is a good ratio for dividing the canvas - is your canvas unevenly divided?

- Do you have boring bits? Cover a section of your

painting with paper and look at it in isolation. Could it stand alone?

- Do you have enough variety or too much? If too much variety get out some gesso or a dark glaze and tone areas back.
- Does it fit with what you have discovered about your own unique style or is there something that needs adjusting? For example, if I create with thick lines I will almost always dislike an artwork! If I correct them to thinner lines, immediately I like the artwork a lot more!
- Look in a mirror - often things will stand out. Also view it upside down.
- Is there a quiet place on the canvas to balance out busy areas?
- Does your artwork tell the "story" you want it to tell?
- Are you communicating the emotion that you want with the colours you have picked?

10. INTENTIONAL STYLE SHEET

1. My colour palette is:
2. The emotions I want these colours convey are:
3. My dominant colour is :
4. My choice is mainly warm/cool colours (circle one)
5. My dominant tone is dark/medium/light (circle one)
6. My artistic style is:
7. My influencing artist is:
8. My composition is :
   C shaped, S shaped L shaped Grid shaped circular V shaped triangular other (circle one)

9. My mediums are:

10. My inspiration/theme is:

11. What I want to communicate is:

12. Soft edges or hard edges dominating?

13. My substrate is paper/wood/canvas/ other (circle one)
    (if you want to sand your art use wood, and if you want to create large think of weight of the artwork, particularly for postage).

14. My format is rectangular /square/circular/other (circle one)

15. Any other intentions................

16. My texture is mainly:

17. My tools are:

18. Other notes:

11. YOUR UNIQUE MARKS

Exercise:

- Create a pattern or mark making mini journal

Tiny notebook 6 ways:

1. A keychain notebook made with cut out shapes of card, hole punced and then threaded onto the key chain

The keychain I used in the example below is attached to a mini zipped bag. This is really useful as you can put more cut out shapes into it as well as a marker for creating on the go. If you are going to do a lot of circular "inchies" the circle punch shown in the image below can save you a lot of time. It is also great if you don't like the circles you cut manually and prefer perfect circles!

2. Tiny notebook accordion style

3. Tiny notebook: no sew style

Use folded pieces of lightweight card and use a

ribbon or elastic band to tie the pages together

It's important to use card and not paper as the firmer structure of the card will keep the book in shape. From my experience, without the card support the book will warp when tied together.

4. Tiny notebook from one page (also called a zine)

Below is an example:

Here’s a demonstration of how I created it:

There is a one page instruction sheet in your workbook that explains how to make a zine. (See chapter 12 if you haven't already downloaded it)

5. Tiny notebook made by sewing a pile of pages together and sticking the outside pages to a piece of card

6. Or you could purchase a tiny notebook

Prompts :

- First page: dots
- Second page: lines
- Third page: shapes
- Fourth page: symbols off your keyboard
- Fifth page: repeating patterns
- Sixth page: pattern from the room you're in. For example; woodgrain off your floor or a cushion pattern or a pattern from what you're wearing
- Seventh page: pattern from nature e.g., leaves

- Eighth page: pattern from music notation

- Ninth page: pattern from alphabet letters (even foreign alphabets)

- Tenth page: pattern from numbers

When you make your marks, they can be soft edged or hard edged. This is determined by your medium.

For more ideas: Use combinations of the prompts above.

By the end of this exercise you should be closer to knowing what marks you like to make and then be able to incorporate them into your art and style.

12. YOUR FREE PRINTABLE WORKBOOK

your free printable workbook link

Sign up to my newsletter list and receive a printable pdf workbook

You can also scan the QR Code below

All the best for your art journey,

Dorothy

ABOUT THE AUTHOR

Dorothy Murgatroyd

Dorothy Murgatroyd is an artist and author based in Tauranga, New Zealand. She can usually be found creating art, reading books or attempting to get to that elusive 10,000 steps by walking her local beach.